THE COTSWOLDS

— THE LIGHT AND THE LAND —

PHOTOGRAPHS BY COLIN BAXTER

DAVID & CHARLES

Newton Abbot　　　London

British Library Cataloguing in Publication Data

Baxter, Colin
   The Cotswolds: the light and the land.
   1. England. Cotswolds
   I. Title
   942.4170

   .ISBN 0-7153-9837-7
   ISBN 0-7153-9938-1 pbk

Printed in Singapore by CS Graphics Pte Ltd
for David & Charles plc
Brunel House   Newton Abbot   Devon

INTRODUCTION

I have always thought of the Cotswolds as quite mysterious, cleverly hidden from the main roads. You can travel right past them on the M5 motorway or through them on various trunk roads without so much as a hint as to why this is one of Britain's special corners. In the right conditions, however - a summer evening perhaps, in warm oblique light - you can catch just a glimpse of the treasures tucked away in amongst woods and fields. Golden church towers of stone (almost the same colour as the light it seems), sit boldly as if they have always been there, with chimneys and roofs around them.

There are other intriguing clues that something more human than the back of the 38 tonne truck in front of you lurks only a stone's throw to the left or right. Signposts with names such as Compton Abdale, Eastleach Turnville or Duntisbourne Abbots - the sound of the names themselves beckons the traveller to turn off and see what more may be found.

More often than not, after the shock of suddenly switching from the bumper to bumper regime of the main road to the delights of a narrow country lane, one rounds a corner and finds rows of delightful honey-pot cottages huddled together in a sort of natural haphazardness. The perfection of some groups of buildings, especially in the setting of the most beautiful villages makes one wonder how they have survived the changes of more recent decades, but thankfully they have.

The real Cotswolds are to be found by wandering and discovering - the unexpected pleasure of the odd lonely cottage, the secluded manor house, the tiny community of a church and its handful of buildings. Meandering through a well known place at quieter times of the year can also be rewarding, if you are lucky.

There was an evening in mid-summer when we found ourselves in the picture postcard village of Lower Slaughter, just after a cloud burst. There was a brief rainbow, then the light turned to gold, transforming the stone to a deep orange-brown and touching the clouds with purple. there was not another soul to be seen except the ducks. It was wonderful.

It is not just the villages, however, that make this a special part of the country. The Cotswolds are essentially an area of high ground, as is clearly evident from the number of impressive viewpoints along its western fringe, commanding panoramic views of the river Severn's path and the distant Black Mountains of South Wales.

Behind this rampart of the west is a plateau, with countless hidden valleys scooped out from its mass. Often heavily wooded on their steep slopes, these 'bottoms', as they are often called, are almost invisible from many of the roads which skirt across the flat top level.

They too wait to be discovered, especially at the moment when light, land and just being there all come together, and create a glorious picnic spot.

It is these little corners of the landscape which make the Cotswolds what they are. There are probably more special places than could ever be discovered in a lifetime and within each one the more you look the more you see. So we will return again, aware that despite our familiarity with the area we will never really know it completely - there will always be so much more to find.

Colin Baxter 1991

THE CHURCH OF ST JAMES, CHIPPING CAMPDEN

TOWARDS ALDERTON HILL FROM HIDCOTE BARTRIM

THE KING'S ARMS, STOW-ON-THE-WOLD

NR BAGPATH, OZLEWORTH

DUNTISBOURNE LEER

HIRONS HILL, NR SALFORD

NR CHIPPING NORTON

CIRENCESTER

13

UPPER SLAUGHTER

WEST WOOD, NR CHARLTON ABBOTS

BROADWAY TOWER

TYNDALE MONUMENT AT SUNSET

17

CHASTLETON HOUSE

18

FERNEY HILL, NR DURSLEY

HAILES ABBEY

COOMBE HILL, WOTTON-UNDER-EDGE

ADLESTROP POST OFFICE

NR KINGSCOTE

HAYCROFT BOTTOM   NR TRESHAM

CHAVENAGE HOUSE

TOWARDS THE SEVERN BRIDGE

NEBSWORTH

DOWNHAM HILL

CHIPPING CAMPDEN   NR FRAMPTON MANSELL

THE RIVER EYE, LOWER SLAUGHTER

LAMPERN, NR ULEY

SCOTTSQUAR HILL, NR PAINSWICK

COLDWELL BOTTOM

ARLINGTON ROW, BIBURY

BROADWAY

BURFORD

LITTLE ROLLRIGHT

NR LITTLE COMPTON

NORTHLEACH DOWNS

TEMPLE GUITING

LOWER SLAUGHTER COTTAGE

BOURTON-ON-THE-WATER

NEWARK PARK, OZLEWORTH

WEST DOWN

VALE OF BERKELEY

CAM LONG DOWN   LOWER SLAUGHTER

WYCK HILL

KINGSCOTE WOOD

THE RIVER SEVERN FROM FROCESTER HILL

NR BOURTON-ON-THE-WATER

ROUND HILL EBRINGTON HILL

HIGH WALL, AMPNEY CRUCIS

CAMP BARN, WINDRUSH

COLN ST DENNIS

SHERBORNE POST OFFICE

STUMPS CROSS

NR GREAT BARRINGTON

WINCHCOMBE

PAINSWICK VALLEY

HILL FARM, CHASTLETON

EYFORD HILL

TOWARDS CLEEVE HILL   LITTLE RISSINGTON

CALMSDEN

NR SNOWSHILL

LOWER SLAUGHTER FARM

BARNSLEY

AMPNEY CRUCIS

EDGEWORTH

FARMINGTON GROVE   SHERBORNE

SPOONBED HILL

STOW-ON-THE-WOLD

NR UPPER COBERLEY

OWLPEN MANOR

RIVER COLN, COLN ST ALDWYNS

LECHLADE

TOWARDS DUMBLETON

SHERBORNE COTTAGE

CHASTLETON HILL

WINDMILL HILL

NR NYMPSFIELD

WINDRUSH VALLEY

WIMLEY HILL

DUNTISBOURNE LEER ROOFTOPS

UPPER SLAUGHTER HOUSE   CUTSDEAN HILL

LANGLEY HILL   SELSLEY

NR COALEY

SUNSET TOWARDS THE BLACK MOUNTAINS

INDEX OF PLACES